Yell and Shout
Cry and Pout

A Kid's Guide to Feelings

by
PEGGY KRUGER TIETZ, Ph.D.

illustrations by

REBECCA LAYTON

I am grateful to my family and friends who:

Encouraged my vision for this book,

Supported me when I was discouraged,

Reviewed and critiqued when I needed perspective,

And loved me all the way through.

What makes you laugh, or blush, or run and hide?
What makes your eyes open wide?

Can you guess? Do you know?
Whatever you feel inside will show.

When something scares you, fear makes you hide.
If you're surprised, your eyes open wide.

When someone is mean, you'll be angry and shout.
If a friend moves away, you'll be sad and pout.

When someone is friendly, you'll be happy to play.
If someone is loving, you'll smile all day.

When an apple is rotten, disgust makes you gag.
If you are selfish, shame makes you sag.

Feelings tell you what's happening to you.

When you feel them inside you'll know what to do.

LEARN ALL THEIR NAMES BECAUSE EACH
IS THERE TO TAKE CARE OF **YOU**.

ANGER

Anger tells us when we've been mistreated
so we can defend ourselves.

Maria and Kim were at the beach building sandcastles. Maria was finishing the last tower on her sandcastle when Kim grabbed the shovel she was using.

"Stop it, Kim!" yelled Maria. "I'm not finished!"

"But I need it," said Kim.

"It's not your turn! You're not being fair!" yelled Maria.

"I don't care," said Kim, and she ran over and knocked down Maria's castle.

"NO!" screamed Maria. She was furious. "Why are you being so mean?" she asked Kim.

Maria's face was red and her fists were tight.

MARIA WAS ANGRY.

Some feelings make you feel tense
and tight like anger and fear.

Sometimes we all
get angry like Maria,
and sometimes we:

Yell and shout

Glare and frown

Stomp around

Start a fight

WHAT DO YOU DO WHEN
YOU'RE ANGRY?

Here are some things that might make you angry

WHEN YOU THINK SOMETHING'S UNFAIR
like someone grabbing your shovel without asking. You'll feel angry because they weren't being fair. Anger helps you stand up for yourself when someone's being thoughtless or selfish.

OR

WHEN SOMEONE HURTS YOU,
like a friend pinching you hard on purpose. You'll be angry because pinching hurts. Anger gives you the strength to push your friend away and make them stop.

OR

WHEN YOU CAN'T HAVE SOMETHING YOU WANT,
like not being able to sleep over at your friend's house because your parents said, "No." You'll be angry because something you wanted didn't happen. Anger makes you speak up when things are important to you

WHAT MIGHT MAKE **YOU** ANGRY?

FEAR

Fear tells us if something is dangerous
and helps us escape.

Carlos was in bed and his big brother Juan was telling him a ghost story.

"And the monster gobbled him up!" said Juan. "The end."

"Don't tell me any more stories!" said Carlos. "I want to go to sleep."

He didn't want his big brother to know it, but the story had really scared him. He had to go to the bathroom and the hallway looked very, very dark. His mom had forgotten to turn on the night light. Carlos started to walk down the hall, but it was so dark he could hardly see anything. He suddenly heard a sound.

"Juan, I hear a funny noise," he called out to his brother.

"It's just the wind," said Juan. "You're imagining things."

"How do you know?" asked Carlos.

"Oh, don't be a 'fraidy cat," said Juan.

But Carlos was sure he heard something. Maybe it wasn't dangerous, but he froze in his tracks. Then he turned around and ran back to his bed and pulled the covers over his head. He heard his brother laughing, but he still was shaking.

CARLOS WAS AFRAID.

HOO!
HOO!

Sometimes we're all
afraid like Carlos,
and sometimes we:

Tremble and shake

Stand very still

Hold our breath

Run and hide

WHAT DO YOU DO WHEN
YOU'RE AFRAID?

Here are some things that might make you afraid

WHEN YOU IMAGINE YOU'RE IN DANGER,

like hearing mysterious noises at night. You'll feel afraid because strange sounds are creepy. Fear makes you extra careful until you figure out if you're in danger.

OR

WHEN SOMETHING REALLY DOES THREATEN YOU,

like a snarling dog leaping at you. You'll be afraid because sometimes angry dogs bite. Fear tells you when you are in danger and helps you get out of the way.

OR

WHEN YOU'RE AT RISK AND MIGHT GET HURT,

like being too close to the edge of a cliff. You'll feel fear because if you fall off, you'll be badly hurt. Fear makes you uneasy until you move to a safer space.

WHAT MIGHT MAKE **YOU** AFRAID?

SHAME

Shame tells us we've done something
wrong and helps us say we're sorry.

Zack sneaked into his brother Caleb's room. He knew Caleb
was downstairs doing his homework. He loved his brother's
collection of toy cars and trucks, especially Caleb's new red
fire truck. Zack had just picked up the truck and started to leave
when Caleb suddenly walked into the room. Zack quickly put the
truck in his pocket.

"What are you doing in my room?" Caleb asked.

"Nothing," said Zack.

"You're lying," said Caleb.

"No I'm not!" said Zack. But his face turned red and his head
hung down as he stared at the floor. He really loved playing with
his brother's truck, but he knew that taking it was wrong.

ZACK WAS ASHAMED.

Some feelings make you saggy and slow
like shame and sadness.

Sometimes we all feel
ashamed like Zack,
and sometimes we:

Turn bright red

Hang our head

Look away

Try to leave

WHAT DO YOU DO WHEN
YOU FEEL ASHAMED?

Here are some things that might make you feel ashamed

WHEN YOU DO SOMETHING THAT YOU KNOW YOU SHOULDN'T, like lying and saying you didn't steal something when you did. You'll feel ashamed because you weren't honest. Shame makes you feel bad until you tell the truth.

OR

WHEN YOU LET SOMEONE DOWN, like not going for help when a bully hurts your friend. You'll feel bad because your friend was in trouble and you didn't do anything to help him. Shame helps you try to be braver the next time.

OR

WHEN YOU DO THINGS THAT MAKE PEOPLE DISLIKE YOU, like calling friends names and making them cry. You'll feel ashamed because you were mean. Shame helps you say you're sorry and try to be friends again.

WHAT MIGHT MAKE YOU ASHAMED?

SADNESS

Sadness tells us when something unpleasant has happened and helps us to get used to it.

One day Josh's mom told him that his best friend Billy was moving to another town. Josh and Billy played together every afternoon until Billy's moving day. On that day, Josh and his mom watched a big moving van drive away as Billy waved goodbye. Josh waved back.

"Why did Billy's dad have to get a new job somewhere else?" Josh asked his mom.

"You'll miss Billy, won't you?" asked his mom.

"I wish Billy could have stayed with us," said Josh.

"That's a nice wish," said his mom.

"Yeah, but he couldn't, could he?" said Josh. He started to cry. "I wish he was still here!" he sobbed. Tears were running down his face.

"You two had so much fun together," said his mom and she gave him a big hug.

"Yeah, no one's as fun as Billy," said Josh.

JOSH WAS SAD.

Sometimes we all feel
sad like Josh,

and sometimes we:

Cry and sob

Mope around

Want to be alone

Can't have fun

WHAT DO YOU DO WHEN
YOU FEEL SAD?

Here are some things that might make you feel sad

WHEN YOU HAVE A BIG DISAPPOINTMENT, like your best friend moving to another town. You'll feel sad because your friend won't be there to play with you anymore. Sadness helps you get used to painful things that can't be changed.

OR

WHEN YOU EXPERIENCE A LOSS, like when your cat runs away and doesn't come back. You'll feel sad, because he used to curl up with you in bed and now it's lonely without him. Sadness gives you time to get used to not having him around and helps you remember how special he was.

OR

WHEN YOU GET LEFT OUT, like playing on the monkey bars with your friends, but they walk off and say, "We're going to play by ourselves." You'll feel sad because you wanted to be included and now you're alone. Sadness makes you cry when you feel rejected. Crying helps others know you need comfort.

WHAT MIGHT MAKE **YOU** SAD?

HAPPINESS

Happiness tells us when good things happen and helps us relax and have fun.

Carmen loved playing baseball. She practiced very hard and always tried her best. Her team was good, because her teammates practiced hard, too. They won so often they got all the way to the championship game. The score was tied when Carmen took her last turn at bat. If she scored, her team would win. She was very excited.

"Take a deep breath, Carmen," her coach whispered in her ear.

She stepped into the batter's box. When the pitcher threw the ball, she hit it as hard as she could. She had never hit a ball so hard. It just kept going and going.

"Home run! Home run!" the crowd screamed. "Run, Carmen, run!"

Carmen ran as fast as she could, all the way around the bases, and slid into home plate. She was tingling all over. Her teammates ran onto the field and hugged her so hard she could hardly breathe. It was like a dream.

CARMEN WAS HAPPY.

Sometimes we all feel
happy like Carmen,
and sometimes we:

Dance around

Laugh out loud

Smile and grin

Giggle and tease

WHAT DO YOU DO WHEN
YOU'RE HAPPY?

Here are some things that might make you feel happy

WHEN YOU'RE PROUD OF SOMETHING YOU'VE DONE, like hitting a home run. You'll feel happy because you practiced hard and really got good. Happiness makes you feel great and proud of what you've done.

OR

WHEN YOU'RE LUCKY, like getting a new bike for a birthday present. You'll be happy because something you really wanted was given to you. Happiness helps you appreciate your good luck and makes you thankful.

OR

WHEN YOU DO SOMETHING FUN WITH FRIENDS, like going to the zoo together. You'll feel happy because it's great to have company when you do things that are fun. Happiness makes you cheerful and friendly.

WHAT MIGHT MAKE **YOU** HAPPY?

LOVE

Love tells us that someone is special
and makes us feel close and caring.

"Let's go!" Kadima yelled to her parents. They were going
to the pet store to pick out a new puppy. "I'm so excited I can't
wait!" she yelled.

Kadima was in the middle of the pet store when she suddenly
stopped. There was a small, brown, very soft puppy huddled in
the back of a cage.

"Here's the one I want," she said.

She reached in and gently picked him up. He looked at her
with big, scared eyes. Her heart melted.

"Oh, he's adorable!" she said. "I think he's shy." She rubbed
him gently behind the ears. Pretty soon he was wagging his tail
and licking her face.

"I think he likes me," she sang out.

"I think he does," her mom said.

"Oh, I just love you," she whispered into the puppy's ear. She turned to look at her parents. "He's going to be the best dog ever!" she said.

KADIMA WAS FEELING LOVE.

Sometimes we all feel
love like Kadima,
and sometimes we:

Cuddle and hug

Whisper and share

Trust and adore

Help and care

WHAT DO YOU DO WHEN
YOU FEEL LOVE?

Here are some things that might make you feel love

WHEN YOU'RE PROTECTIVE AND CARING, like taking care of your cuddly puppy. You'll want to take good care of it because it is special to you. Love makes you gentle and kind.

OR

WHEN SOMEONE DOES NICE THINGS FOR YOU, like when your leg's in a cast and your best friend visits often to cheer you up. You'll feel love because your friend wants to help you feel better. Love makes you feel close to people who show they care about you.

GET BETTER SOON!

OR

WHEN SOMEONE LIKES YOU MORE THAN ANYONE ELSE, like your grandma, who visits and makes a fuss over you. You'll feel love because she adores you and can't stand not having you near. Love makes you feel close and special.

WHAT MIGHT MAKE **YOU** LOVE?

DISGUST

Disgust tells us when something might make us sick, so we can avoid it.

"Mom, I'm hungry!" Linda yelled.

"Have a glass of milk before dinner," her mom told her.

Linda went to the kitchen and poured herself a glass of milk. She took a big gulp before she noticed that the milk was sour. It tasted horrible! She spit it out and it got all over her shirt. The smell was awful. She wanted to throw up.

"Mom, the milk's sour!" Linda yelled.

"Oh, I'm sorry, Linda," her Mom said. "I forgot to buy fresh milk yesterday."

"It's so gross," said Linda.

LINDA WAS DISGUSTED.

Some feelings make you feel queasy
or uneasy like disgust and surprise.

Sometimes we all feel
disgusted like Linda,
and sometimes we:

Cringe and back up

Hold our nose

Cover our eyes

Spit or throw up

WHAT DO YOU DO WHEN
YOU FEEL DISGUSTED?

Here are some things that might make you feel disgust

WHEN YOU TASTE SOMETHING BAD, like sour milk. You'll be disgusted, because spoiled food can upset your tummy. Disgust makes you spit things out before they make you sick.

OR

WHEN YOU SMELL SOMETHING NASTY, like when you step on dog poo with your bare feet. You'll feel icky because it smells horrible and you don't want to touch it. Disgust makes you wash off stinky things before they give you germs.

OR

WHEN YOU SEE SOMETHING SICKENING, like when your brother vomits in the toilet. You'll be disgusted because chewed-up food is supposed to stay inside your stomach. Disgust makes you turn away and close your eyes so you don't throw up, too.

WHAT MIGHT MAKE **YOU** DISGUSTED?

SURPRISE

Surprise tells us when something unexpected happens, so we can be alert and know what to do.

It was Ben's birthday, but he wasn't feeling very happy. His parents weren't going to have a party for him. His friend Dan called and asked him to help build a tree house. Ben had fun working on the tree house, but it wasn't the same as having a birthday party. When Dan's mother said it was time for Ben to go home, he still felt sad.

As soon as Ben left, Dan ran to Ben's house, taking a shortcut so he would get there before Ben. Ben's mother let Dan in and he hid behind the living room sofa. Ten of Ben's friends already were hiding around the room.

Ben walked in the front door. "Mom, I'm home!" he said. All of Ben's friends jumped up and yelled, "Happy Birthday!"

Ben's mouth hung open and his eyes opened wide. Then he saw his aunt holding his birthday cake. Ben was so shocked he was speechless. All he could say was, "Wow!"

BEN WAS SURPRISED.

Sometimes we're all
surprised like Ben,
and sometimes we:

Jump and scream

Gasp and stare

Stop and listen

Wonder and wait

WHAT DO YOU DO WHEN
YOU FEEL SURPRISE?

Here are some things that might make you feel surprised

WHEN SOMETHING UNEXPECTED HAPPENS, like having a surprise party you didn't expect. You'll be surprised because you were getting used to the thought of not having something when suddenly it happened. Surprise catches you unaware.

OR

WHEN SOMETHING STARTLES AND UPSETS YOU, like when a dog jumps in front of your bike. You'll be surprised, because the dog came out of nowhere and caused you to fall off your bike. Sometimes surprises happen so fast you can get hurt.

OR

WHEN SOMETHING NEW DELIGHTS YOU, like tasting bubble gum ice cream. You'll be surprised because bubble gum isn't usually an ice cream flavor. Surprise can make new things exciting.

WHAT MIGHT SURPRISE YOU?

Now you know why your feelings show:
They help take care of you as you learn and grow.

Pay attention to your feelings every day.
They show you how to act and what to say.

When danger is near, they keep you alert,
So you can act fast, and avoid getting hurt.

When things are fine, they keep you at ease,
So you can have fun, and giggle and tease.

Like clouds in the sky, feelings come and go.
They're all inside, so just let them show.

Some feelings make us **Tense and Tight**

like

ANGER AND FEAR

Some feelings make us **Saggy and Slow**

like

SHAME AND SADNESS

Some feelings make us **Loose and Light**

like

HAPPINESS AND LOVE

Some feelings make us **Queasy or Uneasy**

like

DISGUST AND SURPRISE

Note to Adults

I wrote this book as a guide for adults to help children learn about their emotions. Children need help making sense of their emotional lives. They need names for what they are feeling, so that they can tell people what's happening to them. Being able to identify feelings and to distinguish between them allows children to communicate more effectively. It also gives you an explanation for their behavior and an opportunity to offer reassurance, problem solve together, and teach them to manage emotions that seem too big or scary.

Being heard will help children feel understood and accepted. Learning that their emotions are worthy of respect will help them learn to respect other's feelings as well. Current research shows that children who are emotionally competent are more resilient, have better peer relations and do better in school. I hope that this book provides the building blocks for children to learn how to identify their feelings and become more self-aware and self-assured.

Here are some interesting facts about emotions:

1. Emotions evolved over many millions of years to respond to challenges in living and so increase our chances of survival.
2. Emotions are automatic pre-set action plans hard-wired into our nervous system.
3. Emotions are neither good nor bad but, like our senses, bring information about what's happening to us.
4. Each emotion has a range of expressions, from mild to intense.
5. Each emotion has a specific purpose and is triggered by particular events.
6. Each emotion has a unique physical profile (facial expression, internal body sensations and external behaviors).
7. Emotions are designed to be temporary events and, when expressed and acted upon, will dissipate and resolve themselves.
8. Emotions are not dependent on our thinking brain, but when our thoughts and emotions work together, we have the best chance of generating optimal behaviors.

Made in the USA
Charleston, SC
28 June 2013